INVESTIGATING
HEAT

SUPER COOL SCIENCE EXPERIMENTS

 CHERRY LAKE PRESS
Ann Arbor, Michigan

SCIENCE INVESTIGATION

by Sophie Lockwood

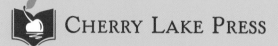 CHERRY LAKE PRESS

Published in the United States of America by
Cherry Lake Publishing Group
Ann Arbor, Michigan
www.cherrylakepublishing.com

Reading Adviser: Beth Walker Gambro, MS, Ed., Reading Consultant, Yorkville, IL

Content Editor: Robert Wolffe, EdD,
Professor of Teacher Education, Bradley University, Peoria, Illinois

Book Designer: Ed Morgan of Bowerbird Books

Grateful acknowledgment to Deborah Simon, Department of Chemistry,
Whitman College

Photo Credits: cover and title page, 4, 6, 7, 8, 11, 12, 13, 15, 16, 19, 20, 23, 24, 27,
29, freepik.com; 5, 9, 10, 14, 17, 18, 21, 22, 25, 26, 28, The Design Lab.

Library of Congress Cataloging-in-Publication Data has been filed and is available at
catalog.loc.gov

Printed in the United States of America
Corporate Graphics

A Note to Parents and Teachers: Please review the instructions for these experiments before your children do them. Be sure to help them with any experiments you do not think they can safely conduct on their own.

A Note to Kids: Be sure to ask an adult for help with these experiments when you need it. Always put your safety first!

Note from Publisher: Websites change regularly, and their future contents are outside of our control.
Supervise children when conducting any recommended online searches for extended learning opportunities.

CONTENTS

The Heat Is ON

How does it feel to sip hot chocolate or another warm drink? How is it different from drinking something cold? Did you know that both **sensations** are caused by heat? So, what is heat anyway? Heat is a form of energy. It comes from the movement of tiny particles called **molecules**. Heat flows from hot things to cooler things. So, hot objects contain more heat energy than cold ones.

Understanding how heat works is science. Science affects your life every day! It is all around you. When you investigate how or why things work, you are thinking like a scientist. In this book, we'll learn how to carry out experiments with heat using things you have in your home. Get ready to make many discoveries along the way.

Getting
STARTED

Scientists often have lots of questions about the things they see around them. They carry out experiments to find answers to those questions. They observe what happens during the experiments. But scientists don't rely on just their vision to learn about something. How does something feel? How does it smell? They make **observations** using all of their senses. Then they draw **conclusions**. Are you ready to think and act like a scientist?

When scientists design experiments, they often use the scientific method. What is the scientific method? It's a step-by-step process to answer specific questions. The steps don't always follow the same pattern. However, the scientific method often works like this:

STEP ONE: A scientist gathers the facts and makes observations about one particular thing.

STEP TWO: The scientist comes up with a question that is not answered by the observations and facts.

STEP THREE: The scientist creates a **hypothesis**. This is a statement about what the scientist thinks might be the answer to the question.

STEP FOUR: The scientist tests the hypothesis by designing an experiment to see whether the hypothesis is correct. Then the scientist carries out the experiment and writes down what happens.

STEP FIVE: The scientist draws a conclusion based on the result of the experiment. The conclusion might be that the hypothesis is correct. Sometimes, though, the hypothesis is not correct. In that case, the scientist might develop a new hypothesis and another experiment.

In the following experiments, we'll see the scientific method in action. We'll gather some facts and observations about heat. And for each experiment, we'll develop a question and a hypothesis. Next, we'll do an actual experiment to see if our hypothesis is correct. By the end of the experiment, we should learn something new. Young scientists, are you ready? Let's get started!

· EXPERIMENT 1 ·

Heat It Up

What do you already know about heat? The Sun provides heat, and so do radiators, stoves, lightbulbs, and your body. Also, some materials change when they are heated. What else do you want to know? What substances react to heat? How do they change? What happens when the heat is taken away?

Let's run an experiment that tests what happens when a substance is heated and then allowed to cool. We'll use four substances: chocolate, a crayon, ice, and sugar. Let's form a hypothesis: **When substances are heated, any change that takes place is permanent.** Let's test the hypothesis!

What happens to ice when it gets warm?

Here's what you'll need:

- 4 pieces of aluminum foil, 3 by 3 inches (7.6 by 7.6 centimeters)
- A piece of chocolate (unwrapped)
- A crayon (unwrapped)
- An ice cube
- A teaspoonful of sugar
- A heat source, which in this experiment is a desk lamp with a flexible arm
- A timer

· INSTRUCTIONS ·

1. Make four pans from the aluminum foil by folding the sides up 0.4 inches (1 cm). Pinch the corners. The pans should look like boxes without tops.

2. Put the chocolate in Box 1, a crayon in Box 2, an ice cube in Box 3, and the sugar in Box 4.

3. Put Box 1 under your heat source. Ask an adult to help you adjust the lamp so the lightbulb is 2 inches (5 cm) above the box. Allow the heat from the lightbulb to heat the box for exactly 5 minutes. What happens to the chocolate? Write down the result.

4. Remove the pan and put it to the side.

5. Repeat this process with each box, making sure that each substance remains under the lightbulb for exactly 5 minutes.

6. After 1 hour, take a look at each substance again. Record your observations.

· CONCLUSION ·

What happened to each substance when it was placed under the heat source? What happened to the substances after they cooled off? The chocolate and the crayon melted. When they cooled, they returned to solid form. The ice cube melted and became water. The sugar did not change because the lightbulb's heat was not hot enough to melt the sugar.

So, our conclusion is that the changes that happen when something is heated are not always permanent. Was our hypothesis correct? No, but that's okay. Scientists get a lot of things wrong at first. Then they come up with new hypotheses to test!

FACTS!

You may have heard people say that it's hot enough outside to fry an egg on the sidewalk. Is this true? The temperature needed to cook an egg is at least 149° Fahrenheit (65° Celsius). Concrete sidewalks rarely get hot enough to fully cook an egg. But scientists are interested in the ways that outdoor surfaces absorb heat. Could the heat absorbed by the sidewalk be used as an energy source, for example? Scientists hope to find out!

· EXPERIMENT 2 ·

Cool Conductors

In Experiment #1, we learned that heat can change substances from solids to liquids. We also learned that these changes are not always permanent. And the heat that melted the substances in our experiment came from a direct heat source: the lamp. However, the air around the substances also got hot and **transferred** heat to the substances. When heat is transferred in this way, it's called indirect heat. We often use indirect heat while cooking. On the stovetop, the heating element heats up a metal pot. And the hot metal transfers the heat to the food. In an oven, the heating element heats the air, and the heated air cooks the food.

We use indirect heat to boil water to make pasta!

To cook food, you put it into containers that allow the even transfer of heat. These containers might be pots, pans, dishes, or plates. Metal, glass, and ceramic are good heat **conductors**. Let's do an experiment and see which surface conducts heat best. Here are three possible hypotheses for this experiment:

Hypothesis #1: Metal will conduct heat better than plastic or wood.

Hypothesis #2: Plastic will conduct heat better than metal or wood.

Hypothesis #3: Wood will conduct heat better than metal or plastic.

Choose the hypothesis that you think is correct.

Here's what you'll need:

- Butter or solid vegetable shortening
- 3 small plastic beads
- Metal, plastic, and wooden spoons (1 each)
- A small, heatproof glass bowl
- A pot holder
- Hot, boiled water
  (Ask an adult to help you boil water!)

· INSTRUCTIONS ·

1. Using a small dab of butter or shortening, stick a bead onto the handle of each spoon. Place each bead at the end of the spoon's handle.

2. Put the heatproof glass bowl on the pot holder.

3. Place the spoons in the bowl so that the handles are above the rim of the bowl.

4. Ask an adult to pour a cup of boiling water into the bowl.

5. Watch what happens. Which bead drops off first? Why? Did you prove your hypothesis? Be sure to record your results.

·CONCLUSION·

The conclusion will vary depending on which hypothesis you chose to test. However, you might have determined that metal is the best conductor of heat. Metals allow heat to pass through them easily.

Metal pots are often used to cook food. Now you know why!

EXPERIMENT 3

Keeping It Warm

Sometimes it's important to contain heat. Materials that do this are called **insulators**. Your winter coat insulates you from cold air. Your home has insulation to keep heat from escaping through the roof and walls. Insulators work by trapping air around the hot or warm substance. The air holds the heat. This heated air is not able to easily move away from the heat source.

But what makes a good insulator? Let's do an experiment to find out. You are going to wrap four coffee cups with different insulators. Which one do you think will work the best? Think about Experiment #2. Which spoons did not conduct heat well? Does that give you a clue? Let's make a hypothesis: **Plastic insulation will hold the heat best.**

Here's what you'll need:

- A page from a newspaper
- 5 identical coffee cups
- Cellophane/plastic tape
- A piece of aluminum foil, 1.6 inches (4 cm) long
- A small plastic trash bag
- An old cotton sock
- Very hot water
- Scissors
- A timer

· INSTRUCTIONS ·

1. Fold the newspaper to the height of the coffee cup. Wrap the newspaper around the cup and tape it so it stays in place.

2. Do the same thing with the aluminum foil and the plastic trash bag.

3. Cut the bottom off a sock and slide the top portion around the fourth cup. If you need to, hold the sock in place with tape. One cup will have no insulation.

4. With an adult's help, pour very hot, but not boiling, water into each cup. Fill each cup to about 1 inch (2.5 cm) from the top. Make sure they all have the same amount of water.

5. Set your timer for 15 minutes. After the time is up, test the water carefully with your finger. Which cup has the coolest water? Which has the hottest water? Write down your observations.

· CONCLUSION ·

Was our hypothesis correct? Did any of the results surprise you? Plastic is considered to be a good insulator. Why? It's extremely slow to respond to a change in the surrounding temperature. Can you think of some other experiments you could perform using various insulators? What is another possible hypothesis you could test?

FACTS!

In the winter, you wear a coat to keep your body warm. You put boots and gloves on. If you aren't wearing these insulators, your body's heat escapes more quickly into the cold air. Based on our experiments, what kinds of materials would make good insulation in a winter coat? What kinds of materials would you not want to wear?

· EXPERIMENT 4 ·

Full of Hot Air

Have you ever seen hot air balloons floating through the sky? They are beautiful to watch. But how exactly do they work? The balloon operator has a heater that heats the air inside the balloon. As the air heats up, the balloon expands. As long as the air in the balloon is hotter than the air outside it, the balloon will rise.

But does heating always make the air inside a balloon expand? You can test this idea by running an experiment. Here are some possible hypotheses:

Hypothesis #1: Air does not expand when it is heated.

Hypothesis #2: Air expands when it is heated.

Here's what you'll need:

- A large balloon
- An empty 2-liter soda bottle, with the cap off
- Duct tape
- A bucket
- Very hot water
- A pair of kitchen tongs

· INSTRUCTIONS ·

1. Put the end of the balloon over the opening of the soda bottle. Seal the balloon to the bottle with duct tape.

2. Put the bucket in the kitchen sink and fill it up with very hot water.

3. Using the tongs, push the bottle into the hot water and hold it there. Be careful! You do not want to burn yourself.

·CONCLUSION·

The hot water heats the air inside the bottle. What happens to the balloon? Why? Did you prove your hypothesis? Gases expand when they are heated. That is because heat gives the gas molecules more energy to move around. The molecules spread out, or expand. They rose into the balloon because the sides of the plastic bottle don't expand as easily as the rubber of the balloon. The air takes the path of least resistance and expands into the balloon.

What does this have to do with hot air balloons? The hotter the air gets and the more it expands, the less dense it becomes. A gas that is less dense will float on top of a gas that is more dense. That is why a hot air balloon always rises as long as the air inside the balloon is hotter than the air outside the balloon.

· EXPERIMENT 5 ·

Hot Stuff

There are many types of energy. Heat energy is called **thermal** energy. Thermal energy is a form of **kinetic** energy. When an object becomes hotter, its molecules move faster. These molecules have more kinetic energy than the molecules in a cooler object.

A **chemical reaction** happens when molecules interact. Do you think that heat affects chemical reactions? Let's design an experiment to answer this question. What do you think the experiment will prove? Let's form a hypothesis: **Heat will make a chemical reaction happen faster.**

Here's what you'll need:

- Masking tape
- 2 clear drinking glasses (use heat-resistant or tempered glasses, which are less likely to break during your experiment)
- A marker
- 1/2 cup cold water
- 1/2 cup warm water
- A small saucepan
- A clock with a second hand
- 2 effervescent antacid tablets (ask an adult to help you find these)

· INSTRUCTIONS ·

1. Place a piece of masking tape on each glass.

2. Use the marker to write "Cold" on one piece of tape and "Hot" on the other.

3. Pour 1/2 cup cold water into the "Cold" glass and put it in the freezer for 5 minutes. You want the water to be very cold, but not frozen.

4. Right before you take the cold water out of the freezer, heat 1/2 cup warm water in the saucepan. Ask an adult to help you. When the water is very hot, but not boiling, have the adult pour the water in the glass labeled "Hot."

5. Open the package of effervescent antacid tablets. Put the hot and cold glasses next to each other. At the exact same time, drop one tablet in each glass. Note the time. Watch the tablets carefully. Time how long it takes for the tablets to dissolve. Make notes about the time. Which tablet dissolves faster?

·CONCLUSION·

Based on the experiment, you might have concluded that the higher the temperature, the faster the chemical reaction. Why is this? If you heat up a substance, its molecules have more energy and move around faster. Because of this, they have more contact with the antacid tablets.

FACTS!

Here's another way of explaining the experiment. When you heat a mixture, you're raising the energy levels of its molecules. That means the molecules move around and bump into each other more often. As a result, reactions are more likely to happen!

· EXPERIMENT 6 ·

Do It Yourself!

Some people power their homes with heat from the Sun. This kind of energy is called **solar**. Solar power doesn't create pollution like energy from coal, oil, or gas. And it's a plentiful and **renewable** energy source!

You have already learned that metal works as a good conductor. Did you also know that the color black absorbs heat, while the color white reflects heat? Use what you know about conductors, insulators, and colors to design an experiment about heating with solar power. First, think about Experiment #1, where you made boxes for heating. You might want to design some type of box for this experiment.

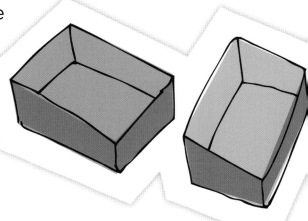

How about testing different colored boxes with substances in them and using the Sun's heat as your heat source? Write up the list of materials you would use and the instructions. Develop a hypothesis, and then run your experiment and write down your observations. As a scientist, you can learn new things and have fun!

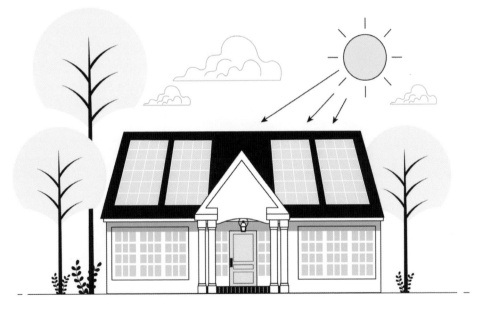

FACTS!

Okay, scientists! You now know many new things about heat. You even learned how to come up with your own hypothesis and test it!

Glossary

chemical reaction (KEM-uh-kuhl ree-AK-shuhn) a process in which two or more substances are changed into one or more new substances

conclusions (kuhn-KLOO-zhuhnz) final decisions, thoughts, or opinions

conductors (kuhn-DUK-terz) substances that allow the transfer of heat or electricity

hypothesis (hy-POTH-uh-sihss) a logical guess about what will happen in an experiment

insulators (IN-suh-lay-terz) materials that slow the loss of heat

kinetic (kih-NET-ik) a form of energy caused by motion

molecules (MOL-uh-kyoolz) when two or more atoms are joined together; these tiny parts make up everything

observations (ob-zur-VAY-shuhnz) things that are seen or noticed with one's senses

renewable (re-NOO-uh-buhl) able to be renewed or replaced by a natural process in a short period of time

sensations (sen-SEY-shuhnz) feelings resulting from something that happens to or comes into contact with the body

solar (SO-luhr) relating to a sun

thermal (THUR-muhl) having to do with heat

transferred (TRANS-ferd) moved from one place to another

For More Information

BOOKS

Batchelor, Jacob. *Energy*. New York: Scholastic, 2019.

Green, Dan. *Eyewitness: Energy*. New York: DK Publishing, 2016.

Kenney, Karen Latchana. *Energy Investigations*. Minneapolis: Lerner Publishing, 2018.

WEBSITES

Explore these online sources with an adult:

Britannica Kids: Heat

Generation Genius: Heat—Transfer of Thermal Energy Video

PBS Kids: Thermal Energy and Heat

Index

About the Author

In addition to writing books, Sophie Lockwood does experiments in her kitchen all the time! Although most of the experiments are called dinner, Sophie and her granddaughter actually did every experiment in this book. Sophie lives in South Carolina with her husband and enjoys reading, playing bridge, and watching movies when she isn't writing.